CHOOSE LIFE

How to Get to Your Next Level and Get Unstuck!

Bonus #5 Winner Keys Action Plan

KIYANNI S. BRYAN

Write It Out Publishing

Kiyanni S. Bryan, CEO & Founder of Write It Out Publishing LLC. Virginia Beach, VA
Affiliates…
Living Word Illustrations, Illustrator – Jason Josiah
All About Business, Editor – Shawn Maynor

All scripture quotations are taken from the Holy Bible, NIV, NLT versions.

ISBN – 13: 978-0692886038

ISBN – 10: 0692886036

Dedications

*For all your prayers, advice, phone calls, encouragement and friendship …
I dedicate this book to you Mom (Elouise M. Bryan-Townsend). Thank
you for your Love and support, I Love you.*

*For my Dad (Gene "Barry" Lloyd), I just want to thank you for how
you encourage me and support me. You believe in me to accomplish what I
set out to do, and I will do just that.*

*For my precious daughter Ryanna, I want you to know that there is no
Dream Too Big to Dream. Pursue them relentlessly and impact every
environment that you enter, with the powerful gifting's God has designed
you with. Love, Mom.*

Acknowledgements

I just want to take the time out to thank one of my closest friends and business partners, Jason Josiah for all your support, encouragement, patience and hours worked on this project. I thank God for you, and Bless you.

For my sisters that covered me in prayer, weathered storms with me and loved me through my transition ... I love you Melissa Jones, Triston Sumpter and Shenequa Mack.

Love to the women in my life that encourage and love me, grandmothers Nettie, Georgianna, aunts Annette, Cynthia, Shirley, Grace, Nancy, Lucinda, Esther.

Love to the men in my life that support and love me, my uncles Rev. David Manigault, Tio (Anthony "Tony" Aromi), god-fathers (James Williams) and James Curney Sr.

To my siblings, KayVonna, Kenneth, Dayvid, Joel, (Leah), Latesha, Jarron, Rashun, Kyalis, (cousin/siblings) Delana, AJ, Latorie, Jamaal, Nika ... I love you all and I want you to never settle but pursue every God given Passion you have.

I acknowledge with love my family, the Bryan's, Lloyd's, Manigault's and Doctor's.

Forward by Dr. Gerard H. Ruff

Into every generation there emerges the bright and gifted minds which help to positively carry that generation forward.

Kiyanni Bryan is such a person in this generation. Her creative and informed approach to living, business and the marketplace set her apart as one to be sought out. It's clear that her gifts of organization and administration influence her writing, but most of all her heart to see others excel is felt in every word she writes. With wisdom beyond her years in this millennial age, she is positioned to bridge the now with the next.

In this book, Kiyanni masterfully helps you unravel the tangles of your heart and mind which can absolutely preempt your life's success. No one is exempt from the challenge of figuring out the "what next stages" of life; this book was written with you in mind.

In my thirty-one years of business and leadership, I've enjoyed learning from those with a story behind their education. It's been the likes of TD Jakes, Joyce Myers, Les Brown and many others that translate life into unpackable tools to live by; I love to hear and read their writings. I believe that Kiyanni is cut from that type cloth, she's gifted in life translation, helping others grasp their lives and futures.

In her book, "Choose Life," the most significant aspect of all is her love of and relationship with God.

This is the glue, the source and the foundation of Kiyanni's writing. When you read this book, you will experience order, clarity, and empowerment. These attributes accompany anyone, who like Kiyanni, spends time in prayer drawing from the supplier of all things good and perfect.

So, if getting to the next level and getting unstuck is what you desire, this is the book for you.

Let's Choose Life!

Dr. Gerard H. Ruff, Pastor & Author

TABLE OF CONTENTS

CHOOSE LIFE

How to Get to Your Next Level and Get Unstuck!

Bonus #5 Winner Keys Action Plan

BY

KIYANNI BRYAN

PREFACE

Do you want to Live or Die?

That was the question I began to ask people when I saw them at a place in their lives where they were stagnant, not growing, idle and stuck in vicious sin cycles where they involuntarily repeated the same mistakes. You would think the answer to that question would be an easy one, or that the response would be a trick answer. It is a very direct question with a very much needed answer; the answer to this question will change the whole course of your life.

Let's lay the foundation for the course of this book by looking at a few vocabulary words. Even when you *Know* the meaning of a word, we can sometimes become so familiar by constantly hearing them, we don't value the potency of the word or grasp them with an in-depth understanding.
You may need to refer to these words as you receive revelation of the truth I am going to share with you throughout this book.

Per the Merriam-Webster dictionary ...

To _**Live**_ means to be alive, to **CONTINUE** to be alive and to occupy a place by dwelling there. The synonyms are: abide, dwell and reside; while the antonyms are: depart, die, expire, pass away, perish and succumb.

**Alive** means to have life, **still in existence**, active in competition with a chance of victory, knowing or realizing with sensitivity, marked by alertness and energy. Synonyms for this are: animate (lively with excitement), breathing, live, living, quick; a few antonyms are: asleep, breathless, cold, dead, deceased, expired, nonliving.

**Die** means to stop living, **to end life in a specified state or condition**, pass out of existence, to check out.

**Survive** means to remain alive after death, continue to function or prosper despite of, withstand hardship. Synonyms are: ride out, weather, make it through; antonyms are: fall, fizzle, give out, go out, run out.

**Forsake** means to give up on or leave entirely, to renounce or turn away from. Synonyms are: abandon, desert, leave, quit.

**Choice** means to decide between two possibilities, select freely, to pick or elect, a preference.

Now, let's use these words in a declaration. Ready, repeat after me…

"I will Live and Not Die, I will not stay stuck in Survival Mode because I am Alive in Christ, so I Choose to Forsake the negativity of my Past and Welcome the New"!!! In Jesus Name, AMEN!

This book is to guide you from the survival mode of merely existing to the liberation and abundance of living life *on* Purpose and *in* Purpose.

SURVIVAL MODE

To live life in survival mode means you are just getting by, complacent where you are, no depth, living life on a surface level; nothing extra, playing everything safe, sticking with only what you know, passing away slowly. You come into agreement with whatever life throws at you and yield your heart to that thing. What is the foundation of survival mode really? You survived a period of your life that was extremely overwhelming; you weathered an incident or set of circumstances that was intended to take you out of the game. The game of life that causes you to approach the new with a different and fresh outlook versus tainted vision that comes by way of pain and torment. Once you made it through that period or phase of your life, you were supposed to transition to your next level but you ended up camping out and staying there.

If you have lived and or are living in survival mode, you have encountered a giant in your life that was such a challenge that dealing with it took the breath out you. You didn't even know or think you would have made it out to tell the story but you DID!!! AND YOU HAVE!!! The basis of those that live afraid in Survival Mode have a root of *Fear* at the heart of it. You have now made it to a place of safety which has become your refuge and safe place. When you feel trapped, stuck and wedged into an idle mode, you grow hopeless and will eventually stop living. In an effort to run away from that pain, you end up running straight into it deeper by pitching a tent and camping out in that place for too long. What you must keep in mind is that you are to always allow the LORD to be your refuge and strength by calling on Him in times of hardship, instead of trying to protect yourself from a place of pain. Let Him comfort you and be your guide. Self-protection is a temporary fix but the covert wings of the Lord will sustain you.

Psalms 46:1 God is our refuge and strength, a very present help in trouble."

God intended "Life" to be something that was intentional. He intended that you would LIVE; not just survive but Live in Abundance and Excess of having plenty. The Bible says in John 10:10 "The thief comes only to steal, kill and destroy; I have come that you may have life and have it to the full." (NIV) Jesus paid a price for you to live and paid the ultimate sacrifice that you may be Free to have life today. It is a gift from God to you, a blessed, filled Life.

Over the years, I have counseled and coached loved ones and friends about the importance of living life past a point of mere existence. I watched how so many, both men and women, were filled with talents, special gifting's, God-given callings and abilities, and they literally refused to live out their purpose in life due to fear. Their fear was of moving out of the current comfortable position they were in and traveling to the unknown place of the new. Satan had done a very good job in convincing them that they would stay where they were and that they should just get comfortable by living in the box with the tight lid on it. In the vocabulary definition above for the word die, it states **to end life in a specified state or condition;** this is very true of those that choose to live in survival mode because the incident that put them in a place of Fear to begin with caused them to HALT life at the state they were in.

THERE IS A WAY OUT!

From all the people that I could influence over the years, to be honest, not ALL of them made it out. That for me was disheartening and I didn't understand it, BUT the Lord showed me the distinct difference of those that didn't make it out and those that did. The difference between those whose lives changed after I shared some infallible truths with them versus those that stayed in the place of being "Stuck" in their life was…. A CHOICE.

The ones that began to experience a better life did so because they CHOSE to do so, while others opted out of the choice to "LIVE" and maintain a binding agreement residing under an illuminating false haven of survival mode. To stay in a place of complacency is you telling God, I DON'T want what you have for me and I forfeit my inheritance as a child of the King. You may be accepting the payment for your sins in salvation but not in its entirety if you don't live the life God intended for you to live.

The Lord revealed to me some time ago that salvation was so much more than not going to hell, as many of us were brought up in church to think. Salvation means to be whole in your mind, your soul, body and spirit which means sane, healed from old wounds throughout your life and with an opportunity to not have infirmities rule and dictate the quality of your life. So, what am I saying exactly? Those that did the work, which were the ones that became more alert and aware of who they were and their surroundings, pressed their way out of the web of being stuck, without excuses, and made it out.

I venture to say that if you Choose Life, by altering your current thought process, forsaking the negativity of your past, meditating on the truth of God's word, repentance before the Lord, walking through strategic plans of implementation and making the word of God your ultimate and FINAL authority…. YOU WILL LIVE AND YOU WILL WIN!!! Let this book offer you a clean slate and opportunity to start over because if there is breath in your body it is NEVER too late to start again.

I pray that the eyes and windows to your soul are open so that the floodgates of God's glory through truth and revelation minister to those deep places. I declare unto you, YOU WILL LIVE AND NOT DIE!

INTRODUCTION

It Takes Courage to Live Past Your Flaws, Never Forget You Are Not Your Mistakes.

For many years, I lived my life in survival mode. I was completely convinced that I would encourage others and impact their lives but my life would never amount to anything. Through my process of growing up from childhood to adulthood, I experienced abuse, rape, sexual assault, neglect, rejection and abandonment. Every possible odd you can think of was against me, including my culture, the projects I grew up in and the poverty mindset I possessed. I had nothing to look forward to, was a mediocre student and had no push in me to give anything more than average. I was always disappointed in myself and felt as if I just couldn't do anything right.

Not knowing what to do or how to handle these deep hurts that went back so far in my life to before I could remember, caused me to do whatever was needed to cope and numb myself so I could function in my life. There were some suppressants I used along the way as coping mechanisms: becoming a workaholic, keeping busy so I didn't have to face the mirror, drinking, partying, smoking and attempts to pursue relationships with different men.

These things were temporary aids to my pain, and made matters a whole lot worse. I had to deal with my issues and in addition was forced to now fight addictions that fed my flesh and began to rule my life. I thought I was in control of it all, but the truth was, it all had control over me and I was very deceived. I was screaming for relief in my life and didn't quite know how to tap into it, nor did I know who could help me get to a place of rest in my soul.

What exactly was I feeling? Feeling like I was stuck in a web, with minimal to no hope of getting out. I oftentimes felt as if I were suffocating in the middle of the day and wished that I could crawl inside of myself and disappear. Thoughts of suicide would welcome me on a regular basis, oftentimes when I opened my eyes in the morning. I would hear daunting noise that sounded like static. My world was so loud and full of turmoil. I was very timid at times, very anxiety ridden, afraid to say what I was thinking and afraid of being rejected by people.

Agonizing fears of people leaving me and turning their back on me was enough to make me quit. I didn't see any value in who I was nor did I really know who I was. The thought of being stuck within itself made me very fearful and it seemed like I could never find the words to articulate to anyone how I felt. I did an okay job at times, as far as hiding my issues, but that was very scarce as I am not a person that hides discomfort or disgust well.

Trying to be an overachiever, a perfectionist and going overboard in attempts to prove that I was worth something went on for so many years that I lost count. I had an appearance of being strong, stable and mentally sound but those times were short lived and met with some type of outburst or a vast behavior that could no longer suppress my emotion. When I couldn't hide anymore, all my steps forward turned into double the amount of those steps backwards and I regressed, constantly slipping back into old habits and behaviors for comfort.

"While in a growing process, staying in the same place past the intended period will cause you to regress."

Years ago, the Lord showed me an extended vision and gave me a deep analogy about a baby in an incubator. The baby was sick and needed to be in the incubator for an allotted amount of time. Over time, the baby began to eat and gain strength while being attended to by medical professionals. Then the time came when the baby was ready to get out; strong enough with a built up immune system that could now handle being on the outside. Instead of letting the baby out, they kept the baby in. They continued to give the baby the same care they had been giving it, such as milk and no cereal. As the baby was aging mentally and growing in the body physically, the emotional side of the baby was traumatized from being in an idle position.

Eventually, the child adapts to their surroundings and mentally degenerates to a state of making their premature state a normal one. When we as human beings mentally camp out in a place that was supposed to be a pit stop, the effects can be devastating and cause massive delay in growth and development. To Be Stuck is to not only to be halted in moving forward but it's reverting backwards. When you revert to something you came from, the grace that was on you when you were there originally is no longer applicable. Going back places you in a worse state.

For example, in the beginning of a school year students are learning new schedules, new teachers and new rules.

They are extended a certain amount of grace for being on time to class, bringing in their materials and doing their assignments. After the first semester, the student should be more acclimated and responsible regarding what they need to do to be functional in their classes. If they carry the same behaviors that they did when the school year first began, they will then have to face consequences because the grace for error that was intended to teach them was not received.

When staying in a place too long you suffer many side effects, such as over excessive vulnerability, sensitivity, lack of sound judgement and reason. You think from a place of only where you've been without any hope of where you can go. Your soul becomes deficient, lacking nutrients and healthy substances that are needed for you to mature.

From this book, you can expect to be encouraged, but also very challenged in your belief systems. I'm going to push you to run forward and not go back, by impacting your thought process with the truth of God's word. You will reflect on situations in your life where you endured pain and strongholds entered your mind, while you were confused and hurting. It may be uncomfortable at times but remember that every beautiful garden had to endure a pruning process. It is very important for you to be self-aware of where you are and where you want to go to achieve genuine success in life, all this starts with your Choice.

Part I
Choose to Win!

CHAPTER 1

The Jar

Adapting to your Surroundings

There is no greater agony than bearing an untold story inside you."

Maya Angelou, I Know the Caged Bird Sings

I remember my grandmother nurtured a bunch of beautiful plants in the living room of her apartment. She watered them, pruned them, talked to them and made sure they got lots of sunlight. She did such a great job that after a while, the plants grew long and high surrounding the windows and the walls of that side of the living room. It was obvious that the growing of these plants would outgrow the space she provided for them. I began to wonder what she would do with them, but she ended up not having to do anything.

When the plants realized that their growth process was halted by the parameters of the living room space, they stopped growing and survived in that space with boxed off growth. That was amazing to me, the plant was able to adapt to its environment very much like animals and humans.

When not provided enough space to grow in your life, you resort to that place of living in survival mode to life in a jar.

Life in a jar is a life full of limitations with self-imposed barriers and mental blocks. It is when your dreams are only as big as the room you are in, and you are unable to envision a future outside of those four walls. You then surround yourself with those that are negative, that don't pursue their dreams, that allow life to pass them by and have minimal to no ambition. The reason I refer to placing limitations on the quality of your life as living in a "Jar" verses living in a "box", is because what's in a box we know is automatically dead.

When things are placed in jars, it has the appearance of life and is very well preserved. People are more apt to be comfortably living in the jar because they can see their surroundings and feel as if they are still in the mix. The truth is the jar is worse than the box, because it carries a form of deception with it. Deception in the aspect of having an outer appearance of being one way but feeling completely contrary within to what your appearance is.

Revelation on Deception – People are deceived by not separating the difference between THEIR will and God's Will. They hold on to what they want and close their eyes and ears to the unction of the Lord via the truth about their situations. They don't fully surrender their will, instead they attempt to squeeze it in the vision or plan to accommodate an ulterior motive. This leaves an open door for the enemy of your soul to come into your life. When presented with the TRUTH, always face your reality and deal with it so you don't have to travel the long and disheartening road of deception.

Count HIM In!

Not too long ago, when I was in a very trying season in my life, the Lord told me REPEATEDLY, *don't count me Out before you count me IN!"* It would be so loud in my ear, that I began to respond back to the Lord openly about what I was hearing.

At that time of my life I was on the brink of stepping into a new dimension of faith. I caught myself battling my "old" mindset and "new" mindset often, meaning that I was being injected with enough faith to change my decision-making but I was always haunted by my past of old behaviors and reflexes. I would think I could do something and then suddenly, that joy or dream was snatched by me trying to rationalize the "How" I would achieve it. I would be in faith for the thing to come to pass, and then immediately lose it by being bombarded with thoughts that I was just kidding myself because those good things couldn't happen for me. I was counting God out of the equation to move on my behalf before I could even really position my thinking to believe that He would come through in my favor.

"Don't Count Me Out, Before Counting Me In" says the Lord

Give the Lord an "opportunity" to show Himself strong in your situation. You trying to figure out the ins and outs of it puts you in a place of resisting the Holy Spirit and prolonging your coming out of that situation. A key to knowing when the Lord has stepped into your situation is when You have taken your hands off it. He will not touch what your hands are on, so when you come to the End of yourself, He is there waiting for you. Then you stand on the promises that He made to you in His word and allow Him to work.

Once the Lord has told you something, or if you wholeheartedly believe that the Lord has given you instruction, you must come into agreement with what you have heard.

When you come into agreement with the vision you are automatically releasing your faith. Faith must be released to come out of the jar to be given room to breathe and go after the impossible. In the jar, your dreams, aspirations and goals are suffocated with no room to grow or flourish. Make the choice to come out of the jar with limited thinking, make the word of God your final authority and begin to step forward.

He wants to Take You Higher

Some years back I had a dream that ended up being an open vision that came to me often. In the vision, I was dressed in what looked to be dance garments packed with mud. I was very dirty and I was walking up this huge set of gleaming white steps. The top of the steps was too bright for me to see an ending, but I knew that the Lord was up there somewhere. The vision would start with me standing on a step that was flooding with water. The next step that I should have taken would have been the next step up to get to higher ground. Instead, I would panic and try to run backwards down the step but when I went to step back on the previous step, all the stairs that I climbed to get to that step were gone.

As I would look behind me I would see a body of water that was so vast, it was the equivalent of a raging ocean that rested behind me. The only thing that came between me and those violent waves was that single step that I found myself standing on. The water that started out only covering my feet went up to mid-calf of my legs. When fear of the water totally gripped me, I could see the hand reaching down to me through the bright light. I would eventually, after squirming for some time, grab a hold of the hand and take the next step up. As I took the first step I would lose a piece of the muddy clothing and the truth of my garment would shine through sparkling white. Then the other foot would follow and although I was on safe ground the waves behind me still made me afraid.

In the split seconds of me squirming, trying to decide whether I was going to go higher and take the next steps on the stairway or stay where I was, several thoughts would run through my mind. This was not a onetime vision, but still, until today, it is something that I see as I mature in Christ. Here is what is happening in this vision. It always starts with me on a step where the water is beginning to rise. This represents when it is time for me to go to the next grade spiritually because I have learned all I needed for that particular grade. The water floods the step to let me know it's time to advance. As the water rises I know that I have been standing there too long. The raging waters behind me represent my past, in which there is no future so I can never go back.

Micah 7:19 Once again you will have compassion on us. You will trample our sins under your feet and throw them into the depths of the ocean!

Out of fear, my reflex was to run back down the stairs to what I knew, to what was comfortable, which is why there weren't any stairs for me to step backwards on. In life, when we become afraid, we attempt to go back to what we know or what is comfortable. But once you come up higher, because you have learned and received new information, you cannot return to a place of voluntary ignorance.

There was another aspect of fear in addition to the raging water behind me. It was the fear of thinking I didn't deserve to advance because I didn't think that I was ready to be in the next grade. The hand coming out of the light let me know that it didn't matter what I thought but God already qualified me. The dirty piece of the garment that was shed and in fact left on the step that I walked off was symbolic of the next step that brought me closer to the Lord. We are made clean the closer we get to the Lord; our sins are washed away through the blood of Jesus.

I'm grateful that the Lord allows this to be a way He communicates with me when it's time for me to move on and come up higher. For me, this vision is confirmation and provides a clear picture of where I am and what I need to do at those times. You may be in a place right now where you are debating whether you should take the next step or stay where you are. I'm here to tell you that you have absolutely and positively Nowhere to go but UP!

The alternative of staying where you are will cost you too much. You cannot afford to waste any more of your life being fearful of moving on nor have regret about what you wish you would have done verses the state of complacency of staying where you were. Whenever faced with a challenging decision of whether to attempt something new or stay where you are, please consider the following two scenarios:

- If you stay where you are currently, how long do you intend to be here? Why do you want to stay? What will you do while in that place? Do you think that this is God's best for you? Will you be personally challenged or stretched in this place? Are you growing? What are your overall life goals?
- If you choose to take the Next step, what are those possibilities? Why has this opportunity been presented? Will you grow in the new place? Will you learn something new? What's the worst that can happen in that next step? Have you been prepared for this already?

These are questions I ask my clients when they make several *valid* excuses as to why they believe that it is too risky for them to move into another dimension. By the time we are done openly discussing the root of those beliefs, while weighing out the pros and the cons, they quickly realize the True risk is staying where they are. They understood that staying where they were would delay their life's goals and cause them to miss potential opportunities to grow.

So, what is the next step for you? Is your next step to a higher dimension attending school to study on that passion you love? A new career? Commitment to a relationship? Possibly separating from a relationship? Writing a book? Or starting a business? Whatever it is, GO FOR IT! Pray and release your faith, because you cannot stay where you are. Choose to permanently destroy the jar and live life in faith without limits.

CHAPTER 2

Words RECEIVED...

Carry Weight

Proverbs 18:21 "Words kill, words give life; they're either poison or fruit—you choose."

As far back as I can remember, I have always been an optimist. I was always able to see the bright side of a situation in the darkest times. It wasn't until I came into early adulthood that I realized my perspective on life's circumstances, because I was finally taught what an optimist was. You would think that being such a positive thinker, life would have been great for me, right? Unfortunately, that is not all the way true.

Although I saw things in life from a positive perspective, I was surrounded by many that did not. My optimism was met with severe judgement, criticism, snickering and pure pessimism by family, friends and loved ones. It's as if they just didn't want to believe that there COULD be a positive outcome, so I was bombarded with worse case scenarios and paranoid based predicted bad endings. It was mentally taxing and frustrating for me, but worst of all, it invoked FEAR into me.

People have always said that the words you speak and words that are spoken to you have great power; I personally have a disclaimer to that. I believe it's the words RECEIVED that carry the most power. Someone can tell you that you are not attractive, and depending upon how you process that information will determine its power. Would you receive that word to be your truth and react with offense? Or, would you reject those words because they do not agree with the Truth you know about yourself which is that you are amazingly gorgeous.

Outer appearance means nothing without the genuineness of inner character.

You have the choice to "Receive" or "Reject" a word. This is a kingdom right to all individuals but rarely exercised due to ignorance. Many don't know that they have this type of dominion because they lack intimacy with God. It is intimacy with the Lord that brings you into new revelations and truth. I have noticed that when this principle is first exercised, it is most commonly attempted when people have become desperate with a desire for a different outcome.

These outcomes pertain to housing, children, finances, death and receiving a bad report from the doctor. It is at those points, when they are more fearful to not petition God than they are to petition God, that many will become daring enough to believe the Lord for the miraculous. I myself became one of those that dared to believe for the impossible.

In October 2011, I was told by my doctor that I needed to have TWO surgeries. One was an endoscopic nasal & sinus surgery, the other an endoscopy orthopedic surgery on my right knee. I was told about both surgeries in a 30-day time period.

Now, I had never really had anything serious happen to me medically before, nor had I ever had to undergo surgery on my body outside of an oral surgery.

The doctors suggested nasal surgery because I had about 5 sinus infections in a 10-month time frame. They stated that it was too many times and that surgery was needed to cure this issue. They explained about possibly cutting the tissues in the nasal area of my face and they shared some of the horrible side effects that were known to occur. (Blank stare) I totally zoned out of that conversation, and asked for my prescription for antibiotics to treat the current infection that I had at the time. I totally REJECTED that information. If I could speak what I was thinking, I would have screamed out loud "THE DEVIL IS A LIAR!" But, I was calm and I was not moved by the report.

Meanwhile, my right knee was constantly swelling over a 2-month time frame. This started out of nowhere and it was very painful. Not long after my knee would swell, I could not walk for long periods of time or wear heels without great pain. I was sent for an MRI the same month of the sinuses report. About two weeks later, I received the report knee surgery was needed because my knee was in bad shape. At this point I'm like, the doctor play too much and I don't think this game is funny, at all. No way in the world I believed I would have surgery, let alone TWO. I began to pray with a different fervency and that always changes and prepares the climate for miracles.

Now, I have a quick disclaimer to share. At the time of all of this happening, I was not so strong in my faith. I was just going back to church from having been out of church and not living for the Lord for over a year and a half or so. The Lord was wooing me and I was being drawn back to His love. I said this to say that I had to make a choice to want to believe God for my healing. This choice came without much preparation or stability in my faith.

A series of events took place in the fall of that year but I stood firmly on the choices I made to believe God to BE God in my life. I ended up going to a Spiritual Gifts Conference the following month in November after my doctor reports. While attending I received what was said to be a miracle regarding my sinuses. I was healed from the current infection, have never had one since then and never needed surgery for my sinuses because those tissues were completely restored. I ended up having knee surgery some weeks later.

That experience changed my life because God used the time I was off of work to pour into me and began to work on my soul. I was finally *Still* enough for Him to really address the deep issues in my heart. That process of my knee surgery was more of a sabbatical than anything and I was also healed supernaturally. What was supposed to take 12 months of rehabilitation, only took 6 months. God honored my faith and it wasn't because I had done anything to deserve it; it was simply because He is *Good.*

Chapter 3

ROOT OF FEAR

1 John 4:18

¹⁸ Such love has no fear, because perfect love expels all fear. If we are afraid, it is for fear of punishment, and this shows that we have not fully experienced his perfect love.

Fear is the main underlying root that hinders our ability to make choices. From the strongman of fear stems many other demons such as anxiety, torment, paranoia, apprehension, dread, dis-ease, terror, horror and distress. The results of these spirits in your life form strongholds such as deep hurt, pain, disappointment, discouragement, loneliness, anger and unhealed wounds. We are focusing on fear because that is the biggest strongman, and is the seed that every bad tree in our life sprouts from.

To be delivered from fear is not a blanket action or just a one-time deal; when you cast it out, it goes away once and for all. There are levels to fear. For instance, I experienced severe times of financial hardship in my life. I mean where I didn't know where the next meal was coming from for my daughter and I.

God provided for us and proved to me on numerous occasions that He is our Jehovah Jireh, supplying all our needs according to His riches in glory. After a while of enduring hardship, the enemy was unable to punk me in that area because there were too many documented instances where God made a way out of no way. So, in the area of finances, fear had lost its grip.

But, in the same vein, while I was dealing with that, I also went through one too many bad relationships; one of them even ended in an ugly divorce. After that, I was afraid to allow God to choose my mate and did not trust God in this area, as if it was His fault. I had to be accountable and accept fault in the part I played by getting married in error. I made a choice to proceed into a relationship with a man knowing that we were unequally yoked, mentally, emotionally and spiritually. I repented for that decision, forgave my ex-husband for the part he played and God healed me from that wound.

In reading Creflo Dollars' book "Overcoming Fear", he spoke about how fear was something on the outside of us that was trying to get in. That revelation gave me a whole new perspective on fear, and going forward I became more mindful of its entry points in my life. Demons enter a person by way of an open door; something that is done by the person that opens them up to demonic activity. This can be a movie you watch, songs you listen to, company you keep, alcohol you drink or intimate soul ties created.

Other entry ways can be out of your control such as someone hurting you, being in an accident, unprecedented events in your life, the loss of a loved one, and physical illness or sickness. Any opportunity given that the enemy can find to attack your soul, he will take advantage of.

He is waiting anxiously to come in and set up shop for fear to get into the headquarters of your heart.

To eradicate the power of Fear in your life, you must meditate on the truth of God's word and focus on how much the Lord loves you. Begin to pursue deep intimacy with the Lord by strengthening your relationship with Him through studying the word, reading resourceful books, watching television programs that encourage, and being around faith filled believers that motivate you. Guard your gates, your eyes, ears, nose and mouth so that you can keep fear on the outside with no entryway in.

A Childhood Reflection

From the age of 12 – 14 I lived in Oahu, Hawaii because my stepfather was in the Navy. Myself and 3 of my friends that lived on Barbers Point Naval Base, had a sleepover which we did often. I don't remember how we got there but we planned to go the beach to watch the sunrise. None of us were from Hawaii; we were all military families and everyone was from different parts of the country. In school, we had heard of a Hawaiian legend that said at a certain time of dawn, on the beach closest to our house, you could hear and see the dead soldiers of the past marching along the beach. Our crazy tails went out there to see if this story was real.

When we went, it was so quiet, empty and chilling. We surely, after being out there for a little bit, began to hear steps on the sand. Eventually, one of my friends had a tube float and we got into the water. At least 3 of us, including myself, could not swim and had no business getting in the water but next thing you know, we were out there. Two of us short, and the other two very tall. We floated and drifted out so far that we eventually went under. I remember thinking I was going to die, and I deserved it. When I awakened, I was on the beach coughing and gagging. I don't know how I was brought back to shore when the undercurrent was pulling us under. The girls and I never spoke about it again, I think we were all too afraid.

The following year, during the summer break, all the kids in the neighborhood walked to the nearby pool. Many of my friends from school were there that didn't live in my neighborhood. We were all having a good time but kids will be kids. I was so nervous at the pool because the boys were throwing each other and girls into the deep end. Being that I couldn't swim, I was terrified whenever they would run past me. Eventually, they threw my friend into 10 feet and they didn't even know if she could swim which was extremely dangerous.

When we were in our last hour at the pool, I finally stepped foot in the water away from my wild friends at the other end. I wasn't standing there for 10 minutes before someone came from the back and pushed me. I went under the water splashing and panicked. After what seemed like forever of splashing and choking on the water, one of my friends told me to stand up. So, I did. (Smiles) I was only in 3 feet of water but I was about 4'11 in height at that time. Traumatic experience for me.

I grew up into my adulthood afraid of the water, and even worse, I made my daughter afraid of the water. It took years for me to get into both pools and beach water, but one day I decided that I was going to try being that my life is in the hands of the Father. I have come a long way over the years by being comfortable in the water. Although I have not learned to swim yet, my daughter has learned to swim.

It is important to know the root cause of how things started, and how to handle those things. Did someone or a situation in your life plant a seed of fear that grew and sprouted into a monstrous tree? Did you experience pain that was undealt with, or endured wounds you don't speak about? Signs and behaviors to look for to know if the demon of Fear is operating in you are anxiety, anger, doubt, mental anguish, oversensitive, paranoid, insecure, feelings of rejection and abandonment, severe worry, judgmental, impulsive, passive aggressive, fear of people's opinions, codependent, pessimistic, jealous and envious, etc.

In prayer, ask the Lord to show you areas of your heart where you need deliverance from fear. Then, use the word of God to attack those thoughts.

CHAPTER 4

FAITH

EXERCISE YOUR FAITH

To exercise your faith, you must be aware and forsake the past but stand on the promise.

The exercising of my faith was on trial in the season of my life when the vision captured on the cover of this book first took place. The Lord wanted to bring me into closer relationship with Him and heal me of things of my past. I realized that it took no special magic or tricks to get to a place where I would just trust God and take Him at His word, but it took a conscious decision to *BELIEVE* in what His promises were without trying to rationalize or make sense of His divine plans. The bible declares that God's ways are not our ways and His thoughts are higher than our thoughts. (Isaiah 55:8-9) We should not be trying to figure out the mind of an omniscient God but more so learn how to heed instruction with obedience to His will for our lives.

I was blessed to have sat under the teaching and ministry of some very powerful men and women in the body of Christ. It was also around the age of 8 that my prophetic gifting began to manifest. So, I was what many consider to be a "church girl".

I had seasons of life that I was in and out of church but overall, it was obvious that God was in my life. Always trying to do that right thing; knew a few scriptures, labored in the ministry, singing in the choir, intercessory prayer teams, prophetic trainings and never missed a Sunday…. but I lacked Faith.

Now, when I say I lacked faith, I mean I didn't know how to exercise my faith. Faith is a muscle. It is something that you must work on daily to maintain strength and victory in your life's situations. I always BELIEVED in God, but belief alone carries minimal to no action with that thought process. There are many things that I believe exist but I do not support. What I support, I apply myself and put action to, meaning faith is a verb and or action word.

Hebrews 11:1 Now faith is the substance of things hoped for, the evidence of things not seen.

How can there be evidence of something not seen? Faith becomes a tangible presence of your beliefs that causes you to move towards a goal. Without faith, there would be no reason to move forward. Faith is the currency that releases your kingdom resources, it is a posture of acceptance to what you believe in. So, if you were a football player and you were in the middle of a game, you should have a posture of open arms to receive a pass. If your arms are not open when the ball is thrown to you, you won't be able to receive it. Faith is the open arms to receive the ball; for you to be ready for it, it must be activated and expected.

A big factor of Faith is "EXPECTATION", you must be expecting. When women are expecting a child in their process of pregnancy, they begin to prepare. They go to doctor's appointments, eating habits alter and they buy things for the new edition to the family. What if a woman that was pregnant did NOT prepare for what she was expecting? I have seen incidents where women didn't even know they were pregnant until they gave birth. How scary is that? In those instances, both the mother and the child were in life threatening situations because there was no preparation due to there not being any expectancy. Sitting in expectation grows your faith, develops muscles within you and opens your mind and eyes to maximize possible opportunities.

STRETCH

In December of 2016, the Lord woke me up in the middle of the night and began to speak to me. I sat up in my bed and grabbed my pen and prayer journal to prepare to write down what the Lord was saying. As I prayed and spoke back to the Lord, He dropped into my spirit for me to go to a conference that was upcoming the following month in Chicago. Now, I knew about the conference and was aware of all the details but had no intentions on going. The reason why is that it was in CHICAGO!!! I reside in the state of Virginia, see the issue. (Smiles) I never have a problem with traveling and love to travel, so that wasn't the issue.

My thought process was more of "how will I afford to get out there?" It was Christmas time and things were already tight financially. I could not imagine how I would possibly get out there and stay in a hotel for those days. As all these thoughts ran through my mind, I said "Lord are you sure?" … to make sure I was hearing correctly. He indeed made it clear to me that I was going to that conference that was in 4 weeks.

I made the CHOICE to release my faith and come into agreement with what the Lord said. I said out loud, I am GOING to the conference.

Later that morning, when I got to work, I looked up hotels and contacted a friend who was believing God to be able to go to this conference as well. She came into agreement with the word of the Lord for me and we prayed together, declaring the will of the Lord. The power of God touched us both and the Lord spoke through her declaring that "it IS so!".

Now, remember how Abraham and Sarah in the Bible were promised a son? (Genesis 21) They believed the promise but Sarah went and took matters into her own hands by having her husband lay with her handmaiden, Hagar. Hagar indeed bore a child, and that child was Ishmael but Ishmael was not the promise. Although God loved Ishmael and he had his own purpose, he was the result of a manmade blessing. Manmade blessings come with a great price because if it was made by man, it must be maintained by man instead of being fulfilled by God and sustained by God.

In my excitement of going to the conference which was decided on a Wednesday, I called a friend and asked to borrow money to pay for the plane ticket as well as pay for the room. I needed it to be done within TWO days, per the info on the website for us to receive the discounted rate. My close friend was in the middle of a financial challenge and told me that he would get back to me. By that Friday, I had not heard hear back from him. I was discouraged and upset that we missed the window for the discount as well as the opportunity to be able to stay in the hotel where the conference was being held.

That Friday night, I cried myself to sleep, not for any other reason except the fact that I was afraid that I would not have the money in time to go. I was even fussing with the Lord, complaining about how none of this was my idea and wasn't even on my mind until He dropped it into my spirit. I could feel the tug of war in my soul, as the enemy was taunting me to CHANGE my confession by blurting something out in anger that would forfeit all the prayers of believing that I was going. It was the vile presence of the enemy I felt to cause me to say something I shouldn't, that made me want to stand my ground the more and believe.

I messed up by putting God on MY time clock. Just because it didn't happen the way I wanted it to happen didn't mean it wasn't going to happen. I have found that the Lord shows Himself in impossible situations, so that He may get the glory. Once I got over my little pity party that weekend, I was back on the wall praying and believing God for me to go on this trip that was less than a month away. Meanwhile, the friend who is a covenant sister of mine that prayed with me, informed me that the Lord told her to cover my portion of the room cost. Look at God.

On Christmas Eve, I had to go out and run an errand. When I returned home, before entering the house, I checked the mailbox and there was a letter from an insurance company that I was an agent for. The letter stated that I had 30 days from the date of the letter to claim the dollar amount of $265.00, or it would be turned over to the state. I was completely stunned, seeing as my plane ticket was $204.00. I had no idea that I had money out there and it was literally almost a year and a half later when I was being contacted. That following week, when I returned to work, I faxed in the paperwork and shortly after received my check in the mail. God is FAITHFUL; release your faith and stand on the word. He can NOT lie and He Does Not Fail. I am a living witness!

2 Timothy 2:13 If we are unfaithful, he remains faithful, for he cannot deny who he is.

To Exercise Your Faith:

- Find scriptures that speak to your situation
- Pray using the scriptures as a focus and foundation for what you are believing the Lord for
- Stand on the word by guarding your thoughts and heart in Christ Jesus, be aware and alert. In times of dismay,

declare the word and make sure you always have on the armor of God. (Ephesians 6:10-18)

▢ Then GO TO SLEEP! You rest and trust the Lord to do what you believe Him to do.

Chapter 5

PRAYING MADE SIMPLE

1 Kings 8:28 Yet give attention to your servant's prayer and his plea for mercy, Lord my God. Hear the cry and the prayer that your servant is praying in your presence this day.

This is the most powerful tool given to us by God, the ability to Pray. It is simply open communication with God but it has various facets and tremendous impact. Time spent in prayer is where you grow intimately with God and get to know Him in a personal way. You humbly expose your heart and speak to God based on the way you feel, where you are in your life and what you need.

Now, I remember a time where praying was not fun at all for me. It felt like a chore on my daily To Do list that I rarely made priority. I felt like no matter what I prayed, or how long I prayed, I was clearly doing it wrong because I felt my prayers were not getting answered. If you find that it is difficult for you to pray or you have a disposition about prayer that is negative, it could be because of this reason. It is very hard to pray and pour out when you feel like it will be to no avail.

Mark 11:24 "Therefore I tell you, whatever you ask in prayer, believe that you have received it, and it will be yours.

There were two main issues that hindered me from praying effectively; religion and doubt.

Religion. When I would pray, I would mimic the way I heard others pray and use terms and sentences that were traditional and ineffective. Although the words said may have been powerful physically, there was no power BEHIND the words because the motive was a mundane ritual making it ineffective. I grew up in a church where the norm was not to speak in tongues but against that norm was my Uncle who was the Pastor and fluently spoke in tongues. This is not acceptable in every denomination, but KNOW that there should truly be no separation amongst believers. As believers, we are to follow the gospel of Jesus Christ, not tradition. Wherever you are, and whatever denomination you are currently in, always seek to please the Lord and never man. Praying in a routine or religious prayers with vain repetition does not allow the Holy Spirit room to move, speak or manifest His presence.

The Bible says that the Holy Spirit intercedes for us and prays on our behalf when we don't know what to pray. (Romans 8:26) When praying, you want to pray in your native language as well as in the spirit. If you have not received your gift of a heavenly language, which is tongues, ask the Holy Spirit to FILL you and then wait on Him to do it. You may receive it instantly or it may take some time, but it starts by asking.

There is power that comes by praying in the spirit and I like to call it our love language with the Lord. Praying in tongues, according to 1 Corinthians the 14th chapter, is direct language between you and God. (If you are unclear on what speaking in tongues is, please study the 14th chapter of 1 Corinthians along with the book of Acts. Remember to ask a trusted pastor or teacher of the word for clarity and understanding. They should also be able to walk you through the process of receiving your valuable warfare tool, which is your heavenly language).

Doubt. Not being in genuine relationship with God made my prayer life very weak. I didn't pray very often and when I did I was very frantic because it was an emergency by the time I did pray. I needed Him to show up, immediately, in a desperate way, because of whatever challenge I was facing at that time. Typical of many, to call on God only when we need Him and place urgency with a time limit on that need. I'm very guilty of that myself so I understand, and because I understand please hear my heart on this. To be effective in prayer, we must pray from a posture of surety, authority and expectancy. We don't have to beg God in prayer for things He already said belong to us; we are to RECEIVE our inheritance. In order to pray without worry, you will have to get to know who God is; you simply cannot trust who you don't know.

It takes trust and genuine relationship to not doubt while in prayer, worrying your prayers are not effective. When you are worrying, you are in a posture of fear and subconsciously not fully believing what you are praying. Here is a Secret I have learned pertaining to prayers that move mountains. After you address the spirit of doubt, by deliberately binding it and casting it out with the authority of God, you align your thoughts with this simple truth. You pray and…

Rule OUT the Possibility that He Won't Show Up!

Yes. Don't let it even be a thought of "what IF", but more of a mental positioning of prayer that says… *because I have come to you Lord and acknowledged you in all my ways, you have to show up! Even if it doesn't go the way I planned for it to go, please make it WELL with my soul because you are HERE with me"*. This heart posture comes with time but will come.

Luke 1:37 For nothing is Impossible WITH God.

How Do I Start

I found it easier to pray when I came to the knowledge and revelation of knowing what FUN things are actually taking place. So many things are taking place when you pray; many things are forfeited by not praying. You can avoid many headaches and regret by allowing the Lord to direct your path and guide you through your daily decisions.

The Lord wants you to ask Him what you should do, and be a lamp unto your feet and light unto your path. (Psalm 119:105) He is with you always, ready and waiting to guide you and steer you into a victorious life. You may be thinking now, but how do I hear from Him? There are many things I can say about how to hear the voice of God but I will make this simple. The Lord speaks to each of us individually, in His own way. Just like relationships, over time the communication will be more fluent and become more natural. Until that time comes, when you feel more comfortable and concrete in the fact that you have heard God give you clear instruction, you must utilize your resources.

Use resources made available to you to access God and the things of God by taking in more of Him on a regular basis. Increase your spiritual diet to develop an appetite for the things of God, so you can be more sensitive to receiving from Him. You should attend church because it's in church that you learn, are accompanied by other believers, and have an opportunity to serve. Church is very important. I won't stay on this topic too long but I will have to touch on it and leave you with some information to ponder. I know that many are deceived to believe that they can worship God from their home and not attend church. Truth is, those that believe this concept oftentimes don't live a *lifestyle* of worship or holiness which is what God has mandated. You don't have to be perfect because He is, but you do have to be surrendered.

Is Church Really Necessary

So, imagine this. You decide that you would like to pursue a degree in Psychology. You get excited and execute the decision by selecting a school to get the education needed and then you register. You go through your process of admissions, introduce yourself to the professors and then buy the books to get started. But then, when class starts, you don't attend. Instead, you stay home and read all your textbooks on your own. Since you are unsure of what you are reading and don't have clear understanding, you fall back from reading at times because it can become overwhelming.

When feeling overwhelmed, you then occasionally go back to class because in class you FEEL better and have a better sense of what is going on. You get the shot or fix you need and then you are off again, trying to homeschool yourself on materials and information you are not knowledgeable of. You make it okay and feel fine, until the tests come. When the tests come, you fail them and it places you in a worse position than you were before you registered. Doesn't sound like a good investment, does it?

This is synonymous of you attending a church service, getting saved at the altar, meeting some of the people at that church and then disappear. You only attend church on national holidays such as Resurrection Sunday or New Year's Eve, and for occasions such as funerals, weddings and a baby christening. Going to church when you are overwhelmed, feeling down and defeated is okay because the church is a spiritual hospital for the sick in body, soul and spirit. It becomes NOT okay, when you only go to have an emotional one night stand with God, at the altar, to get all you need but with no intentions of building relationship. When life's challenges and tests come, will you be able to pass? When you attend church, you are receiving revelation from the pastor/preacher, which is when God reveals His mysteries.

You are surrounded by sisters and brothers in the body of Christ that encourage you and love on you. I don't know how many times that it was congregation MEMBERS after or before a service, that ministered to me so powerfully that I was immediately changed. You are being encouraged, you are offering a sacrifice with your worship and you are connecting in strength with the body of Christ. It is very important to stay connected so that you are covered in the spirit and protected.

Now that we have practically gone over why it is so important to attend church, make sure the church you choose grows you, stretches you, teaches you and encourages you. You should have a healthy conviction that arouses your heart to change and be in tune with God. In addition to Sunday services and Bible studies you may attend, there are other nutrients you can receive throughout your week that will give you spiritual strength. Some ways you can build your spiritual diet is by listening to trusted and credible men and women of God via T.V., YouTube, Periscope, Facebook and live conferences. There are also Christian blogs, websites with great articles, and amazing books by some anointed generals in the body of Christ. By filling yourself up with these substances, you will receive clarity in knowing when the Lord is speaking to you and how to respond to those instructions.

(Feel free to contact me at Activateme.org for more info, I will provide you with some resources I use and trusted ministries that are credible.)

What's Happening Here...

When you are praying, the following is occurring:

- Shifting the atmosphere
- Employing angels to go work for you
- Building up your faith
- Humbling yourself before the Lord
- Developing intimacy with God
- Taking you out of yourself (often deep reflection of self can lead to depression or getting stuck)
- Getting clarity and understanding on your current situations
- Receiving peace
- Receiving strength
- Receiving healing in the physical body and in your soul; emotional healing
- Receiving an impartation
- Receiving protection
- Being restored
- Positioning you to a place of power and authority
- Bringing your heart and mind into alignment with God
- Creating your future

I bet you didn't know so much was taking place, did you? I had no idea at first either.

If I did I would never stop praying. The Bible says pray without ceasing, meaning that prayer should be a lifestyle. (1 Thessalonians 5:16-18) I used to think in order for me to pray I had to be on my knees, hands up in the air, on the floor in my closet to really be considered as praying. That isn't so. There should be quiet times of devotion between you and the Lord but really you can talk to Him all day long. I talk to the Lord in the car, in the grocery store and especially when I need a good parking spot. (Smiles) The point is that over thinking is stopping you from having conversation with the Lord and He loves to hear from you.

Now let's meditate on the following scripture. I particularly LOVE the Message Version of this scripture because it not only makes it clear on instructions we are to follow but it acknowledges how we *Feel* when we are at this place of worry and anxiety. I underlined and bolded the places where you should really let those words sink into your heart.

Philippians 4:6-7 Do not be anxious **or worried** *about* **anything**, *but in everything* **[every circumstance and situation]** *by prayer and* **petition** *with* **thanksgiving**, *continue to make your* **[specific] requests** *known to God. And the peace of God* **[that peace which reassures the heart, that peace]** *which transcends all understanding, [that peace which]* **stands guard over your hearts and your minds** *in Christ Jesus* **[is yours]**.

Isn't that AMAZING!!! If you understood this scripture you should be completely excited. Why did I place so much emphasis on this? Because in order to get *Unstuck*, you have to meditate on the Truth in prayer. You must forsake those feelings of anxiety and worry that you have grown accustomed to and lean on the Lord to receive a different outcome.

When praying, here are some things to consider;

- Confessing your sins – helps you clear your heart (1 John 1:9)
- Repent – get clean before the Lord and stay unstained from the world (Acts 3:19)
- Gratitude – showing thankfulness and appreciation changes focus from bad to good (Colossians 3:16)

- Direction – ask the Lord to guide your steps and present to Him your plans if any (Psalm 25:4 - 5 / Psalm 16:11))
- Understanding – ask Him for clear vision and wisdom (James 1:6)
- His Glory – in your devotion time, let the goal be to enter into His presence (Exodus 33:14)

Prayer is how you enter into a place of rest in the Father, rest meaning peace and liberation. You will go through life and endure storms for sure, BUT a lifestyle of prayer rooted in relationship with God determines if you go through Life with OR Without Him. That Choice is Yours.

Chapter 6

MINDSHIFT

Let's go onto the battlefield.

"The greatest weapon against stress is our ability to choose one thought over another." William James

One of the greatest wars you will ever fight is the one in your mind. It is in your mind that you process external information and turn it into an internal perspective. It is your thoughts that you think about repeatedly, that turn in your soul and infiltrate your spirit. You must be conscious of your thoughts and the external sources they are coming from. Identify the voices that you are hearing by determining the possible outcome or results.

If the end result puts you in a trying position or takes you out of alignment with God, you can figure that it's probably the enemy of your soul or your flesh talking to you. The Bible says you know a tree by the fruit it bears, so you want to make sure that the thoughts you are thinking align with where you want to go in your life. (Matthew 7:16)

Once a decision is made in alignment to His will for your life, grace to achieve that choice is released. Whatever you choose, whether to live or to die will be active in your mind.

As that choice is active in your mind, all your actions, behaviors and eventually your heart will line up with that choice. What goes on in our mind is like follow the leader; the thoughts you think usher you into every emotion and perspective. If you choose *LIFE*, all your choices will subconsciously be in alignment with all the things that give life. An example of this is furthering education, trying that new business venture, forgiving someone that hurt you or even finding a fun hobby. IF you choose death, then you won't seize opportunities. You will feel like life is passing you by which causes a lot of regret. You will carry hurt and be jealous of others prospering. You won't try your best in life and you will settle for whatever is thrown your way.

To go deeper into choosing death, I want to give an example of my home town of Bronx, New York. I grew up in the projects. Project life was all I knew until my teen years. For about 3 years I lived in other states. I ended up moving back to New York to graduate high school and go on into young adulthood. In my projects, there were so many different types of people, all special in their own way, but I will just break them down into two main categories targeting the teens and young adults that chose Life and those that chose Death.

Those that chose life got up every morning and went to work with a positive attitude, smiled on the way to the train station, and didn't cause any disturbance; you barely knew they were around. They kept to themselves with a bold and evident focus that they had somewhere to go and somewhere to be. These students went to school with the expectancy of learning more. It was already embedded in their minds that getting as much knowledge as possible would not only get them to college but get them out of the only life they knew in the projects.

These young people, to include myself, chose to *LIVE LIFE* and all our decisions, behaviors and attitudes boldly reflected our goals and pursuits.

Many of my friends and loved ones, chose death. They didn't care much about learning or expanding their minds. If they went to school, it was for reasons that had nothing to do with bettering their future. They barely considered their future and only lived life from day to day, never taking into consideration possible outcomes that would end up hurting them in the long run. They were violent, negative and to me what I could always see was they were deeply hurting. Their vile acts were a cry for help in a loud, raging storm where everyone was trying to fend for themselves and could not hear them.

They were people that didn't know how valuable they really were and ended up perishing for their lack of knowledge. (Hosea 4:6) Some of my nearest and dearest loved ones and family went to jail, turned to a lifestyle of the streets and drugs and some died. When I look back over all our conversations and choices we made, I realized that there was ONE main choice that begot all the other choices behind it. That choice was about the future, whether we could see one to live or if we were so blinded and discouraged by our current situation that the *default* of not planning for our futures, and only living in the moment, they chose to die.

Your thoughts can usher you into a place of fear or a place of joy, to a place of depression and sadness or to a place of jubilee and laughter. If the brain is not able to function properly the rest of the body cannot function, but it is possible to be brain dead and still be alive per your heart beat. Those thoughts, when they are in the mind long enough, travel to your heart and make the heart sick

Out of your heart flows the issues of your life and tells a story that you can never articulate with words. That's why the Bible instructs us to guard our hearts because it is very precious; YOU are precious cargo. (Proverbs 4:23)

What you believe to be your reality is where you will end up. If you don't want to end up there, keep your mind on where you want to be and go. It is not easy to forsake the negativity of your past but it is mandatory for you to move forward. You won't be able to do it by yourself, nor will it be an overnight success, but now you know that when you CHOOSE to live the amazing life you desire, there is grace and anointing released in your favor to assure that you will be able to do what you are striving for.

This is going to take a *deliberate* focus and effort to shift your mindset and discipline, from self-preservation to depending on God; going from defensiveness to trusting in God, from isolation to being in the company of true Believers; from the mindset of poverty to the knowing of abundance, from the posture of just existing to the joys of living. It is all an active and conscious work to get to your expected end.

Luke 6:45 A good man out of the good treasure of his heart brings forth good; and an evil man out of the evil treasure of his heart[a] brings forth evil. For out of the abundance of the heart his mouth speaks.

Be empowered to know that you always have a choice. Whether it's a good or bad choice, it's a right that belongs to you. I'm telling you to step out on faith. You will never know how truly great you are, how far you can go, how powerfully impactful your life has been, how intelligent you are, how much you are adored, how much you are needed and how much you can really achieve until you TRY. You must step out and Try.

The trials you face today are forming muscles in you that can only be flexed by you lifting the weight. You need muscles to carry you through your next season of life, to prepare you for where you are going. Your hardships, when you go through them with the right perspective, will develop endurance and determination within you that cannot be shaken. This is needed to fulfill your purpose and to reach your destiny. Push, lift, stretch, flex. The pain is temporary, but the results are forever.

IT WAS A TRICK!!!

Now, I want you to pay close attention to what I am about to share. While some of it you may have heard before, it may challenge your perspective. Over the years, I have seen two types of people that struggle deeply with the ability to Choose Life. There are many people that go to church EVERY week with NO manifestation of any change, spiritual growth or maturity. They act and behave the exact same way they always did when they first began attending church. Even if they were raised in church from youth to adulthood, they are still bound by the same demons and engage in the same frivolous behavior showing no evidence of a relationship with God. This group attends church just to say they went so they can get a tick mark for the week for good behavior, or worse, they just go to have an emotional one-night stand encounter with God. They get what they need and roll out.

Then there is the group of people that are so very deep and in-tune with God on a personal level, they don't even go to church. They go on special occasions and holidays, but they are content with church on television and most times not even that. This group of people openly confess they are spiritual and believe in God but not to the point of conviction to obey what God has required of us. The Lord wants us in the company of likeminded men, women and children to comfort us and encourage us. There should never be lone rangers in the body of Christ. Those that are alone and isolated are easier snuffed out by the enemy, like a stray sheep outside of the pack. The disclaimer is there are seasons you may encounter where the Lord may pull you out of a church for a time to transition you and minister to you intimately. If you should face times like this, make sure that it is the Lord speaking to you by checking your deep motives, spending time in prayer and Godly counsel. In this example, I'm referencing more towards those that believe they can have a genuine relationship with God without seeking Him or fervently pursuing Him.

Matthew 6:33 33 But seek first his kingdom and his righteousness, and all these things will be given to you as well.

It is extremely important that you get to know who God is on a personal level and not get caught up in the act of "playing church".

The Lord is looking for a genuine surrender in your heart and you can only Choose to *Live* by Choosing **Him**. He is life and everything outside of Him will wither and die. It is only God that can sustain you, heal you and carry you through this journey that we call life. He is a loving Father and there to hold your hand all the way through. God's intentions for us are great, just like any loving parent would have for their children. In both groups of church people that I mentioned there is one big common factor, DECEPTION.

Last year I was in my kitchen, where I often talk to God and I begged Him "Father, please never let me be deceived". I didn't want to ever come to a place thinking my right was left, and my left was right. I would be dead wrong in a situation and couldn't see it but think I was so right that I would defend my wrong to the bitter end. I saw what it looked like up close and the damaging effects of it to relationships and opportunities in life.

The Lord spoke to me and said, "Deception comes in when there is something within the person that they won't let Go. If they don't turn it over, deception has a grand entry-way into their mind, heart and life." I had to then process that. While trying to grasp what I'd heard, I had an open vision of a 180 -degree protractor that is used for math in school. I saw what looked like a person turning very slowly, literally millimeter by millimeter towards the left. Each time they turned it was because they Heard the truth but Rejected it by holding on to their own frame of mind and thinking. Eventually, they were turned all the way left and their back was to God who was 180 to the right. Their back to the father was symbolic of a reprobate mind.

The scary part was they had no idea they were out of alignment, or detached from God. When the image of the person I was looking at turned all the way to the right, it was drastic and swift. A complete about face occurred, and it was a result of the person deeply repenting. The Lord was showing me repentance gets you back to the feet of the Father. There is still healing that must occur from where they been but their attention is now fully turned to the Father for guidance and love. The choice in that situation was repentance.

Whenever the truth is presented to you, it is your choice to receive it or not. Scientifically so, it is easier to receive a negative comment than a positive one, so people have a hard time accepting truth because it is either too good to be true or it's painful to face. Receiving the truth will keep you from being deceived. In everything you do, there is a choice that you must make.

People that go to church waiting on what I call the "Big Bang" to hit them, are entertaining a form of deception. My interpretation of the Big Bang theory is that people will go to church and wait for a feeling to hit them to cause them to give their lives over to the Lord or to find a church and stay in it. If the decisions are always based on a feeling, it will be easy to slip into places you shouldn't be in as well as not leave places you should leave. We want to be guided by the Holy Spirit and we want to be consciously aware of who we are and what is happening around us.

1 Peter 5:8 [Be] *sober, be vigilant; because your adversary the devil, as a roaring lion, walketh about, seeking whom he may devour:" (KJV)*

It is a trick of the enemy to make you think that you are not an active participant in your life by not owning your choices and being intentional about what it is that you want. In everything you do there is a choice, you choose to get out of bed, you choose to eat, you choose to bathe, you choose to work, you choose what clothes you put on, you choose to smile and you choose to love.

EVERYTHING, is a choice, even when there are minimal options, it is still a choice. In order to accomplish your goals and dreams you must put your hands to the plow and WORK towards your desired end. Every step you take must be intentional and on purpose. The cliché' of "it is what it is", is the cry of bitter and hurt people who carry deep regret. They feel as if they had no control over the things that happened to them in their lives so they begin to rationalize it with a perspective of trying to make it normal in order to function.

The truth is, when God is leading and guiding you, He will lead you into all truth. He will tell you what to avoid and how to stay away from certain situations. It doesn't mean that everything will be perfect and you won't have any issues because walking through issues becomes ministry for someone else. It IS to say that you are only living life to a minimal capacity by not involving the creator of life in your choices and decisions.

CHAPTER 7

SHALOM

HIS PEACE

"Standing outside in the cool of the day, I am facing this river that spans across about 50 feet. The water is gently flowing downstream, not rough water but a powerful body of water with strong currents. On the other side, I see beautiful shimmering green grass, butterflies fluttering around, the air looked brighter and the peace of God was resting in that atmosphere. I tried to walk to it but was then reminded of the stream that was wide and deep, I could not swim and had no boat. I became frustrated as to how I was going to get to the other side of the river, and without there being any words spoken I knew that getting to the other side meant I would rest in the Shalom of God."

That was an open vision I had repeatedly in a season of my life some years ago; I was in the process of learning how to trust God and exercise faith. The other side of that river represented peaceful rest in my spirit that would have come by believing that God would do everything He promised me He would do. The peace of God is the result of intimacy and relationship with Jesus. It is an anchoring in your soul that has you positioned to live with the resolve that the Lord has you. His peace is a gift to you and allows you true rest in your soul and mind. He gives you clarity and removes the clutter out of your spirit, His peace is a fruit of His presence. (Galatians 5:22-23)

YOU CAN'T TRUST WHOM YOU DON'T KNOW...

To have peace assuredly in the promises of God, you must first know the promises of God. My personal definition of the Bible is that it is a book of our ancestors that walked through life, had obstacles, fell short, made mistakes but did not quit. Those trailblazers paved the way to liberty and by their testimonies they let us know how very human we are with our personal ups and downs. With all they endured they were persistent, consistent, strong and had a heart for God. So, when we study the Bible, because we don't just read it as if it were some type of fairy tale book, but we study because it is the most important history book we could ever possess, we should try to identify our own personal characteristics in the testimonies. When you can identify with the word of God it then becomes alive in your spirit.

We are to study the word to show ourselves approved as well as write the words on the tablets of our hearts. When you read, let it be with an anticipation to receive revelation. (2 Timothy 2:15, Joshua 1:8) The revelation that you receive from the Lord, which is information that the Holy Spirit reveals to you, is what changes your countenance, and ultimately your life. The apostles, prophets, evangelists, teachers, pastors, ministers, disciples, new converts and followers of Christ in the Bible that made it to glory, all had this in common regardless of whatever they did…. they surrendered a pure HEART to God. We learn from them, we honor them and we heed their instruction.

Whenever the Lord tells us to do something, it is for our good, even when we can't see it or don't feel like it. As a child, did you want to do everything you were told to do? Did you like chores, missing parties with friends, going to bed early or having to come in before the street lights came on? I personally didn't like any of it, myself. (Smiles) But, as a *mature* adult, can't you see how much it was needed. The emphasis on mature is because it is not an overnight process for people to respond to life's situations in a mature stature. This takes time and personal development to be able to handle things accordingly. Doing those chores taught you how to take care of a home, missing those parties kept you out of trouble, going to bed early made you responsible with rest and coming in before the street lights came on saved your life.

One of the national anthems I heard in my home growing up when I questioned "WHY" I could not do what I wanted to do was …" BECAUSE I SAID SO!". Am I the only one? I wasn't given an explanation at all, just a direct order. This seemed extremely unfair but that too is for protection because children shouldn't be bogged down with the weight of adult responsibilities. So, no matter how much they do not comprehend or understand, they are to obey, willfully trusting that we as parents or guardians have their best interests at heart.

Philippians 4:6 Do not be anxious about anything, but in every situation, by prayer and petition, with thanksgiving, present your requests to God.

When the Lord is commanding us to "Trust" Him, it is really to our benefit. When we trust Him, it is a deliberate tradeoff for our "worries" and "burdens". If we are holding those things, we won't have peace and our souls won't be at rest. When we trust the Father to take care of us, it is a form of Rest. We are basically letting Him know that we will no longer toil, lose sleep or stress over what we have no control of; we willfully hand it over to our Savior. (1 Peter 5:7) Trusting God is so much easier said than done but must be done. Trusting God is not a blanket statement, nor a one motion gestured occasion. Trusting the Lord goes in layers and different segments of your life. It is very normal to have trust in some areas. If you think about those areas you don't worry so much because in those areas the Lord has already proven himself to you.

To really trust Him, you must KNOW Him. Would you trust someone with your heart, secrets and fears that you did not know? This is no different. I can't be overly spiritual with you about this because it will keep you bound in your thinking that you can trust God and not know Him intimately for yourself. I wrote a blog post on "How to Cast Your Cares on the Lord – 7 Ways that will Help", providing practical steps on what to do and how to accomplish this goal realistically.

Link to Blog Post:

http://myprocessblog.net/home/how-to-cast-your-cares-upon-the-lord-7-ways-that-will-help

Learning to trust the Lord takes time and grows just like any other relationship. What is for certain is that if you desire Him, He will show up and meet you right where you are.

Proverbs 3:5-6 "Trust in the Lord with all your heart and lean not to your own understanding, in all your ways submit to Him and He will make your paths straight."

CHAPTER 8

He Loves You

1 Peter 4:8 Above all, love each other deeply, because love covers a multitude of sins.

Without trust or faith in God, you cannot move forward. These components are the basis of what you need to implement the Keys to accomplishing success God's way. The core of being able to have faith in the Lord and to trust Him enough to take Him at His word is to know that you know, that you know, that you know… He Truly Loves You.

I mean really loves you; more than life itself. For many, it is hard to receive these words because they may have an idea of what true love is but they were never shown true love. God IS in fact love and to not have Him makes it literally impossible to experience the most powerful healing antiseptic known to mankind… LOVE. Love is medicine, it speaks every language. It is its own language and goes across every barrier. It softens hearts, cleanses minds and closes wounds. It covers all and rules all. Below is the standard of love, per the truth, which is the word of God.

1 Corinthians 13:4-7 Love is patient, love is kind. It does not envy, it does not boast, it is not proud. ⁵ It does not dishonor others, it is not self-seeking, it is not easily angered, it keeps no record of wrongs. ⁶ Love does not delight in evil but rejoices with the truth. ⁷ It always protects, always trusts, always hopes, always perseveres.

The unfortunate truth is, the world we live in, the majority of the time, does not display these components. Many people, including our loved ones, family members, associates and some friends, mirror the very Opposite of the qualities that God told us is the fruit of His love. So, because we have lived through situations and circumstances with these people from our youth through adulthood, we now question not only what love is but does it genuinely exist. The answer to that is a RESOUNDING YES!

There are people that have been healed, delivered, set free and carry the love of Christ on the inside of them. It is okay to ask God to surround you with those that will love and support you. If you have been hurt, disappointed and or experienced betrayal… especially at the hands of those that are *supposed* to be there for you and love you; it's time to release forgiveness. I know I should have warned you about this but if I did, you may not have made it to this page. Another sure-fire way to get STUCK in your life is to harbor unforgiveness and hold grudges. These are deliberate ways to place barriers between you and the Lord. Forgiveness is necessary because it frees you, and forgiveness is to include forgiving yourself if need be. So, I have good and bad news. Which would you prefer first??? Well, I am going to place two points below.

Read them in whichever order you like.

- Everyone that has ever hurt you, you must forgive them so they and YOU are released from that yoke of bondage.
- Forgiveness is supernatural, in meaning this isn't something you can do on your own. Give it to God by making the choice to forgive; He will meet you there and do the rest.

(The secret is the bad news was first, but the good news should have taken away all the pressure.)

A revelation revealed to me by the Lord, changed my life when He downloaded into my spirit at a time when I was crying out to Him. He let me know it was true, that I indeed loved Him and always had since I was a very little girl. But, it wasn't my love for Him that would save me, it was me RECEIVING His love for me that would ultimately heal me and make me whole in salvation. It is in the act of receiving everything Jesus died to give you where liberation takes place. You must openly receive God's love; you don't want anything to hinder that or step between the two of you.

Jesus is God the Father in an earth suit. He came to earth to do what He knew we could not do, knowing every mistake we would make, and every time we would fall… He STILL chose to love us and to make us His own. Take rest in this, no matter what you have done, there is nothing that you can do to make Him stop loving you. His love is unconditional and He made a choice concerning you.

In the garden of Gethsemane, when Jesus was praying in preparation for being betrayed by Judas and arrested by the chief priest, He asked God if there was ANY other way to do what He was about to do so God could free him.

He finished that prayer with saying, "nevertheless let your will be done". (Matthew 26:36-56) On cavalry, at the crucifixion, Jesus at any time could have called for angels to come down and avenge him but instead he suffered and then He turned His life over to death. They didn't take His life, He GAVE His life. (Luke 23:46) Why? Because of You! He so adores you, and wants the very best for you. He has seen all that you have been through and He has been there for every tear you've cried. In the times you felt most alone, is when He was the closest. He is loving and He is gentle; He is your beginning and your ending. He will never leave you, nor forsake you (Hebrews 13:5); His love is everlasting and when He saved your life You became an investment.

The love of God covers every sin and when you confess your sins, by faith, receive His forgiveness as He has promised. (1 Peter 4:8, 1 John 1:9) The foundational choices that you make that lead you to living a blessed filled life is to **Step 1** - BELIEVE that Jesus loves you, **Step 2** - Trust Him at His word and **Step 3** - have Faith which is showing that you are fully persuaded into Step 1 and 2. Sounds so simple, like it's too good to be true right? But it is that simple. It all starts with a CHOICE. Whatever choices you make in life, your actions, voluntary AND involuntary, consciously and subconsciously will follow those choices.

Legacy

Proverbs 22:6

Start children off in the way they should go, and even when they are old they will not turn from it.

I remember in my early 20's, when my daughter was born, I was at a very reckless place in my life. I survived challenging seasons and had transitioned over to a mental space of settling for the fact that if I have to live in pain, I may as well have fun doing it. I didn't have high regard for myself or the choices I made… started getting tattoos, piercing my body, partying hard and running through toxic relationships. I kept myself very busy so that looking in the mirror would be easily avoidable and I wouldn't have to face what I had become. I was stuck in survival mode and figured while I am young, I will enjoy life to the fullest with no regrets. This mentality was horrible and deeply inherited by a world that wanted to justify reckless behavior so they can feel warranted in their activities. The opposite is true, you are not "living life" to the fullest by not considering your future; you are setting yourself up for destruction and creating a consequential timeline of regrets.

My daughter came at a time where I had taken a series of blows to my heart due to repeated abuse. In this same period of time, I experienced my first broken heart in a relationship, from someone who was at that time the love of my life but not my daughter's father.

In the summer of 2003 I caught the flu, had to leave work early and go to the doctor. When I arrived, and took all the preparatory tests and answered questions by the nurses, I sat patiently in the waiting room, hoping they would give me some medication to feel better. I realized that while waiting, other names were being called and I was skipped in number by a few people. Eventually they called my name, but it was by the GYN side of the hospital.

Completely lost and not thinking, I went and spoke to a doctor who gave me a hospital gown and told me to undress. I thought, why is all this necessary for just a bad chest cold. We go through the appointment and at the end of the examination she tells me, "well… you do have the flu and you are about 5 to 6 weeks pregnant. I went from shock to tears in a matter of 3 minutes, because I mentally processed, in those few moments, that out of the 3 prior pregnancies I experienced, this one was going to happen. The doctor sees my reaction and says I assume that this was not planned, so here are your options. She gave me several methods of terminating my pregnancy, then told me to schedule an appointment at the front desk for the follow up.

As I stood in line, waiting my turn at the desk, I heard a voice say, "go to the elevator". After hearing this voice loudly in my ear about 4 times, I go and awkwardly walk to the elevator and pushed the button. When the elevator came, someone behind the desk called out to me and said "mam, we can help you here… mam, you are next". They thought I had grown impatient and left from anger. Puzzled by my own behavior, I ignored them and got on the elevator.

I was hearing the Lord speak to me loud and clear, and He said, "She belongs to me". I was told right then I was having a daughter, even though I picked out boys and girls names over the next few months. The Lord told me that my child belonged to Him. By the time, I got to the first floor, walking through the foyer, I could hear them calling my name over the loudspeaker. I never looked back and kept walking out of those doors. I found it weird that a clinic I was completely new to went above and beyond to schedule a termination appointment, to the point they were trying to chase me out the door for it. Also, I was extremely amazed at how I could even hear God at all because of the way I was living my life at that time.

In a nutshell, I ended up giving birth to a big beautiful baby girl, putting myself in counseling a few months prior to her being born, cleaned up my life, went back to church, became more responsible, relocated and began to chase God with everything in me. I knew that in order to grow and cultivate what was in this beautiful God given child, I would have to CHOOSE TO LIVE. I would have to heal, and reposition myself. I loved her more than I loved myself. My love for her kept my mind until my heart was healed to the point where I could finally love ME and see myself the way God does.

My love for her kept me from making choices that I knew would compromise her. I made a choice to CHOOSE HER

LIFE by adjusting my living habits. For parents to live broken, hurting and in pain is very selfish to the children. They model, they follow, they see, they hear, they glean, they learn and they mimic. To be a parent you should be selfless.

It calls for sacrifice; you do what's best for them and the Lord will honor you. If YOU aren't really Free, your children won't be Free. Every big process of deliverance I have experienced, my child was delivered from the same spirits within 24 to 48 hours afterward. When those bloodline curses are addressed, they break within you and go down to the generations after you. Once you experience it, you can administer it to protect the legacy of your lineage and Choose Life for your children.

Work Toward Your Desired Outcome ...

Here are some practical examples. I currently have a teenage daughter who was one of the captains of her cheerleading team this year and I am ridiculously proud of her. She made the choice to try out, then she took it further and said I want to be a captain. Both occurred, because she chose to pursue what she desired and was then recognized by the school as an "athlete." She decided to shift her decision-making based on her goal. She didn't consciously do this but it is exactly what she was doing. So, when some of her friends were being a little too loud in the hallway, she dismissed herself and left them there. When she had opportunities to go places she shouldn't or behave in a way that the crowd was behaving, she opted out. Why? Because the goal in mind that she chose was to be an athlete and this meant she was held to a higher esteem of being a model student. She followed that choice by encouraging others to do right and in turn, all of her choices fell in line with her desired outcome.

What is your desired outcome? Where do you want to be and where do you want to end up? It's important to have goals and have accountability for those goals. You want to be very clear on what you want so that you can meet those standards. If you don't know what you want and don't have goals to aim and reach for, you will live life by trial and error.

Take some time now and lay your heart before the Lord. Talk to God about whatever is on your heart and ask for guidance and direction towards sustainable goals. Sometimes worship music, or quieting my space helps me with this process.

Visualize where you are and where you want to end up. Grab a pen a paper and dream. I want you to envision the end result of what you want to accomplish, see it and then write it out. You have to see it in your mind before you can see it

Habakkuk 2:2 the LORD answered me, and said, Write the vision, and make it plain upon tables, that he may run that readeth it.

PART II

Put Your Hands to the Plow

First Partaker of the Fruit

2 Timothy 2:6 "The hardworking farmer should be the first to receive a share of the crops"

Strategy Keys to Implement

You must be completely intentional about your efforts to live the life God intended for you. The Bible says that without "Faith" it is impossible to please God (Hebrews 11:6). Our whole foundation of a relationship with Him is based on faith. Many believe but belief has no action, no movement and no effort. It is your faith that moves mountains, and places you in a supernatural realm to allow the Lord to have His way in your life. (Matthew 17:20)

Now that we have laid a foundation of the importance of our choices by being injected with faith, we can take some action steps to begin to transform our thinking. God is concerned about your current heart condition and wants you healthy and whole. Let's go over some powerful keys to get you started and posture you to Win.

Winner Key #1 – Self Awareness

"Being self-aware is not the absence of mistakes, but the ability to learn and correct them". Author Unknown

I know when you looked at that word self-awareness, there was something in you that shook. This word is frowned upon from many but embraced by those who are exhausted with life as they know it and want a change. Self-awareness takes true maturity and courage to implement. This means that you can evaluate yourself honestly and identify your true character. Self-righteousness is when we can only boast about ourselves with all the good but not be humble enough to acknowledge our faults. (Jeremiah 17:9) When you look in the mirror, or should I say IF you could consider the mirror…. Are you pleased with what you see?

For many years, I could not look at myself in the mirror because what I saw was so far from what I wanted to be. I had dreams of who I wanted to be by a certain age and specific accomplishments I wanted to achieve, but the reality was that I had not positioned myself to receive those desires. Situations in my life, that had occurred over time, made me angry, bitter, resentful and jealous. I needed time to heal from pain so that I could see clearly. As difficult as it may be to share that part of my heart, I want to be honest so you know that where you are, is a common place for change.

Change comes when a situation has run its course. Whether good or bad, the situation has come to a time of shifting and the change is necessary for advancement to an expected end. So, when did your change occur? At what point did you realize that you began to feel like you weren't progressing?

SELF AWARENESS EXERCISE

Identify the major changes that you have experienced in the past 12 months. Then do 5 years and then 10 years. Try to place a date if you can.

These changes can be new additions to the family, new job, loss of job, relocation, death in the family, tragic accident or health concerns. Anything that occurred that impacted you in a great way, even if it was a normal part of life. Take some time to think about it and write down those highlights.

_____

_____

_____

_____

_____

_____

_____

_____

_____

_____

_____

_____

_____

_____

_____

_____

_____In almost all cases, 99.9% of the time when a person traces back to a specific focal point in their lives where growth has stopped… the root was fear. The job of fear is to steal, kill and destroy you. It causes apprehension, dread, stagnation and complacency. Does that sound familiar? Satan is the author of fear and uses fear along with its cohorts of torment, anxiety, panic and frustration to literally halt you right where you stand.

You might say, well I don't think that anything scared me that I can really pinpoint. Let me mention a few emotions that are produced from fear: anger, depression, frustration, abuse, rage, forgiveness, jealousy, envy, skepticism, over-analytical behaviors, low self-esteem, lack of confidence, contentment and unable to dream.

Those are just a few symptoms to look out for to know that Fear is involved with your decision- making. The Bible says that perfect love casts out fear. When we receive the love of God, the power of Fear is eradicated. (1 John 4:18) When did you allow fear to creep into your heart and infest your mind with lies? What incidents led up to you doubting who you were and all that God said you would be? This is key to your growth.

Take a good look at yourself with as much honesty as humanly possible. Get accountability partners that you can trust and that genuinely have a heart for you. Grab a journal and begin to write out incidents and situations that left an imprint in your heart so you can lift those areas before God. Writing things down brings an awareness that can't be denied. While going through this process, memories will be triggered and sensitive areas will be uncovered, but stay prayerful and press through. Take ownership of your faults because you can never overcome what you don't admit exists. This process of being real with yourself in a new light is not an easy process but remember this, God reveals to redeem so address those issues and press forward.

Winner Key #2 – Humility

It takes humility to reach the deep things of God, to enter the holy of holies, naked in spirit before the Lord. There is a true humbleness of the heart that pulls back layers of opinions, quiets personal desires and silences thoughts of insecurities. Humility presents your heart to the Father with a foundation of surrender from your will in exchange for His. You can die to yourself and make your top priority to please Him, with full acknowledgement that without Him there is no You.

Humility is the key to deliverance, and deliverance is needed to fulfill destiny. A heart must be humble to receive the mercy, healing power and love of the Lord that is ushered to the soul in deliverance. It is a place of brokenness that cries out in desperation of a true touch from the Father. A place where pride would drown because of the weariness of trying to repeatedly correct yourself and be self-reliant as well as self-sufficient would be too much pain to attempt again. As a great word of advice, I was always told by my mother, when you are sick and tired of being sick and tired you will do the unimaginable.

The brokenness of your heart is an acceptable sacrifice to the Lord and lets Him know that you are truly sorry. Have you ever entered the presence of God and began to feel like you just wanted to apologize to Him for all you have done wrong? You didn't feel a need to justify your actions or feel that you were as right as you thought. You didn't even care about being right, you just felt the weight of what you are carrying and it caused you to feel very apologetic before God. That is a normal reaction. In His presence, our spirit man automatically knows that we are in error and in that place of His presence our flesh can't be glorified.

Pride is an enemy to growth, prosperity and kingdom success.

It prevents you from hearing, receiving and learning, which are all mandates for your relationship with the Lord. To have the attitude that you don't need any help, and can fix yourself is an act of pride. Not wanting to ask for help or admit weakness in any form is an act of pride. Pride is a cover up of insecurities, fear and fragileness of the heart. It is a protective barrier that protects the infection of the heart and guards the heart preventing the sickness to come out and healing to come in.

Something I always thought about happened in the book of Genesis, the 3rd chapter. When Adam and Eve sinned, they ran to hide themselves in the garden. When God came looking for them He said, "Where are you?". (Gen 3:9) Now, God is omniscient meaning He knows EVERYTHING so why would He ask Adam where he was as if He didn't know where he was? I believe it was to allow Adam an opportunity to humble himself and confess to Him in a state of brokenness. He went to look for him in the place he should have been and called his name to give Adam an opportunity to be cleaned by saying Lord here I am and this is what happened.

Aren't we like Adam in some form or fashion? We know we have issues, we know we messed up but we try to hide it with excuses, cover-ups and casting blame. When Adam was confronted about his mistake he blamed his wife! (Gen 3:12) He didn't take accountability for his part at all, no ownership which showed pride was present. Adam tried to justify his mistakes instead of owning up to them, these actions placed barriers between him and the Lord.

Think about it this way for those that are parents or when dealing with our children. When we KNOW, our children have done something wrong, we still ask them what happened. We give them a chance to explain their perspective and admit to anything if they need to. When they knowingly deny any action we know they made, the consequences they will endure are determined. When they admit to wrong and have remorse, the punishment may be grounding a day or two. If they deny it and make excuses without seeing any fault or hide to try and cover it up, chances are they will do it again. To prevent that, the consequences have to be a little sterner to ensure they learn a lesson. That punishment then becomes 2 weeks with a conversation of what took place. Even though our kids are children and learning, this is all about humility.

The contrite heart the Lord is looking for is a sign of remorse that acknowledges you know you did something wrong. What we don't acknowledge can't be healed, so when you cover it up you become deficient in your soul. Your soul becomes weak, feeble, overly sensitive, infected, fragmented and lacking nutrients. Humility before the Lord is an entryway to submission to His perfect will. Give Him ruler-ship and Lordship over your heart, removing yourself from that throne because there is only room for Him.

HUMILITY EXERCISE

Open your heart to the Lord and share with Him the things that are weighing heavy on your heart. Yes, He already knows but when you speak it out to Him in your prayer time, it will begin to free you and is an act of turning it over to Him.

Winner Keys #3 – Acknowledgement and Repentance

You acknowledged that there is a barrier that you feel you cannot quite break through. You took the first mandatory step which was to admit that something is wrong. Now that you are aware that something is wrong, what do you do from here? You fully acknowledge the truth of how you got to this place. Any responsibility that you may need to take, go ahead and take it. Any decisions you made that you knew deep down in your soul weren't right but you went ahead, closed your eyes and did it anyway... face it. If you willfully sacrificed your relationship with the Lord by attaching yourself to anything or anyone that you knew had the POTENTIAL to separate you from His love and voice, repent.

Repentance is key to liberation in Christ.

Let's look at King David; he wasn't by any means a perfect man but he was honored by God. Why? Why was this man who committed adultery and then sent his mistress' husband off to a battle to be killed so loved and honored by God? David was a real man that had real issues stemming from his bloodline. He dealt with real problems and battled lust. No matter his mistakes, David was still blessed and he is responsible for writing the biggest book in our Bible. What was so special about David???

He had a *REPENTANT* heart! David's heart before the Lord was soft and pliable, even though he battled with his own flesh and needed deliverance, the favor of God was on David.

David was a humble hearted man that didn't make excuses or try to justify his wrongs but understood that ONLY God could heal him and make him right. He loved the Lord and acknowledged His power and majesty. One of David's strengths was that he was a worshipper! He knew how to get to the feet of God! He knew how to touch the heart of God! He knew how to get the attention of heaven with his praise and worship! David unapologetically danced before the Lord and could care less about his reputation. (2 Sam 6:14) The Lord sat on the throne of David's heart, and even with his shortcomings, David had the victory. He never let what he was going through stop him from acknowledging God as the Lord of his life. The God of creation that you serve is a perfect God so He doesn't require You to be perfect; He does require your heart to be surrendered and pliable for Him to access it fully.

ACKNOWLEDGEMENT EXERCISE

Take some time and ask the Lord if there is anything in your heart that is blocking the reception of His love to you. Is there anything you need to openly repent before God about? Write them down, ask the Lord for forgiveness and ask Him for a strategy to not do it again.

1 John 1:9 If we confess our sins, he is faithful and just to forgive our sins and to cleanse us from all wickedness."

_____

_____

_____

_____

_____

_____

_____

_____

_____

Forgiveness. Who are the ones you need to turn over to the

Lord so that you can genuinely forgive them? Those that may

be a part of your life when you can't cut them off or throw them away. You have to encounter them but when you do there is an underlying feeling in the pit of your stomach of rage mixed with hurt. Those people must be turned over to the Lord. Know that forgiving them does not mean that you are putting yourself in a place for them to continue to hurt you. They may not be trustworthy and it is okay to adjust the nature of those relationships; make sure you exercise Godly wisdom in your dealings with them. Even if you can't trust them, you CAN trust the Lord so give them over to Him so you can be free from the situations. Your only job to is surrender them to the Lord with a desire to forgive. The Lord will meet you there and the rest He will take care of.

_____

_____

_____

_____

Winner Keys #4 – Positioning and Posture

These key places are an important role in your being connected to the Lord and your being where you are supposed to be when you are supposed to be. There is such a thing as a Kairos moment, a moment in time that is perfect to its purpose. God is the God of ultimate timing and releases things to you in His timing. One of my favorite songs in church when I was a little girl was the song sang by gospel singer Dottie Peoples, "He may not come when you want Him, but He will be there right on time…. He's an on-time God…Oh, Yes, He is!"

As a child, I didn't fully understand what that song meant. I really loved the song because one of my favorite grand aunts would sing it from her soul. As I got older I realized that to know that the Lord IS indeed an "on time God", you would have to be placed in situations where you were forced to be patient while awaiting the manifestation of His presence. You had to endure some type of trial to know that He was trustworthy and that even though you thought He should have come at a certain time, He didn't come on Your time but He came ON TIME.

When I think of positioning I think of a football game. Now the first disclaimer is I don't fully understand football but learned a little bit about it last year when my daughter became a football cheerleader for her junior high school. It has always been confusing to me and my commentary states that there are a bunch of guys, that take off running when the whistle blows to catch the one guy with the ball but then about 7 seconds later everyone falls on the floor. (Don't judge my commentary.) What I notice is that players are placed strategically at certain points to guard the main player with the ball.

The spiritual war that we are in requires strategy and positioning. That ball is synonymous to your purpose and it must be guarded and protected by the angels and promises of God. Satan has your whole life on a whiteboard in his domain and plans strategies to destroy you, as soon as he is given the opportunity. He knows your weaknesses and plans subtle but powerful attacks to hit you in the areas that are sensitive, vulnerable and worst of all … not healed. What happens when you attack a place that is not healed? The wound is reopened to infection and greater pain than before. You must be positioned in a place where you are alert, ready to move, and sensitive to the commands of the quarterback. (See, and you thought I didn't understand the game lol)

It is important to have a strategy and a game plan of how you are going to reach your destiny. The keys of positioning and strategy are about the planning of the plays, with consideration of the enemy's tactics against you. In reviewing your past, what areas are sensitive to you and doors of the house of your soul need to be closed? Being self-aware, as we talked about earlier, comes into play right about now. It is important that you know yourself, the schemes of your opponent and the goal you are striving towards to formulate a good plan.

Like football players that intercept the ball, they run out and open their arms wide so they can catch the ball. Catching that ball is your blessing of Purpose. You fought to get to it and with all of your might, you run out to catch what you have worked hard to get to and what God has ordained for you. You cannot catch that ball with your arms folded or if you are standing still on the field not moving without much energy.

One of the enemy's tactics is to disappoint you so much that you fall into a place of depression from the oppression, which diminishes your expectations. You become accustomed to things not working for you and subconsciously you begin to welcome the discouragement. Some of the symptoms of those affected by this is when people are skeptical, they say things are too good to be true, they don't believe good can happen to them and they believe the hearts of people are automatically impure. They have a defeated attitude and speak negatively, as well as respond to all situations cynically claiming the worse. Your attitude determines your posture. You would have to have an attitude that is anticipating a positive outcome, that is full of hope to catch your ball of Purpose.

REPOSITIONING EXERCISE

List 5 things you can start this week that will posture you to hear God more clearly, to expect something good to happen to you and to change your negative words to positive words. Make sure these steps are practical and something you can see yourself being able to do. Tag in a close friend for accountability if you like and make it fun, maybe even a challenge with your friend. Remember that good days are ahead of you, just begin to LOOK in the direction that they are coming from. There won't be an overnight change but it starts here:

1. _____
2. _____
3. _____
4. _____
5. _____

Winner Keys #5 – Engage the New & Organize Your Life

All my life I have been an optimist. I know now that God designed me this way because it wasn't taught; I was born this way. I have always seen the glass half full instead of half empty. In my eyes, to deal with my extremely challenging life situations, I had to learn to see things with a hint of Hope and a possible GOOD outcome instead of automatically writing it off to be a bad one. Although this is a gift given to me by God, it is achievable for anyone.

We often ask God for the New but we don't seize opportunities or make any effort to embrace new situations. The engagement on your part to pursue new opportunities is faith. Hebrews 11:1 declares, "Faith shows the reality of what we hope for; it is the evidence of things we cannot see." (NLT) Per the word of God, you begin to engage and pursue as an active step toward the evidence which you cannot see. You must step out and do things that are outside of your comfort zone; extend yourself and get out of mundane routines. Go out and meet new people, be available for conversation to share about who you are and what you do. You are valuable to the kingdom of God and in any event, know that no matter what, someone can always be blessed by your testimony.

GET IN ALIGNMENT TO GET TO YOUR NEXT LEVEL, TIME TO GET FOCUSED!

To be Focused is to maintain full attention towards a topic of interest or goal by keeping it in your focal point with precision and sharpness. It is fuel to your daily activities and takes a front row seat in driving your thoughts and behaviors. Being laser focused propels you forward to your desired goals and helps you gain ground or territory in your perspective area. You must be clear on what you want so you can formulate a vision. That vision will give you an outline on what your focus should be. Your focus will vary through life your life's seasons, but you should always have a focus in front of you.

Remember, in order to be effective and stay motivated, you must complete a thing. Feeling the sense of achievement from completion of your projects is what will propel you to aim to accomplish the next steps for your life.

3 Ways to Align Yourself in Expectancy

1) Prepare. When a woman is carrying a child, she has to align herself to prepare for the birth of that child. She has to go to doctor appointments, take prenatal vitamins, make sure she eats properly and rests. In addition, the family may think of baby names and set up a nursery to prepare for the new bundle of joy.

There have been cases where women have given birth to children and didn't even know they were pregnant. Seems unbelievable but very possible and has happened. That can be deadly for both the mother and the seed, to walk through that process without any awareness of what is about to take place. The birthing can cause shock, trauma and emotional distress.

If you are reading this, I'm telling you that you are pregnant with purpose. Something great is on the inside of you that wants to come out. It is vital to properly prepare for the birthing of your purpose to ensure that it grows up healthy and strong. Preparation is one of the major keys to success.

2) Change Your Mind. It's important to value your past but you will have to leave behind every negative impact that caused you to stumble and hinder your growth. You will have to keep what grows you and leave behind what halts you. Change your thoughts so you can look ahead with anticipation of a positive outcome.

3) Take Action. When you are wishing for something to happen, you may have a deep longing but do nothing about it. Begin to move forward so you don't live with regret and be haunted with the thoughts of "what if". Work on turning your wishing to tangible actions of Faith that is fueled by the focus of anticipating good Hopes of something greater.

Expectancy gives birth to purpose and desire, but you must put Feet to your desires to get to the next level in your life. It really takes faith to live life in expectancy. You become alert and aware wanting to seize opportunities and identifying how to maximize moments. Build up your faith by taking in information that gets you motivated, encouraged and excited about what you are looking for to take place.

Many people that have hope and often wish for things to happen think they are living in a place of Expectancy, but they end up stuck in the same place for long periods of time and don't know why.

PRACTICAL STEPS TO MAINTAIN FOCUS

Begin to turn your time over to God and allow Him to be the manager of your time. While you are in this place of feeling stuck, begin to revamp your life and get things in order. Create a schedule that will enable you to prioritize your time with God, time to take care of your normal responsibilities, time to invest in yourself and time to cultivate your calling. Usually, the environment you live in reflects what is in your mind. If you live in clutter, you probably don't have clarity of thought.

Organization and structure creates an order that brings peace. Chaotic environments breed confusion and fear so you want to be intentional about your time and beware of the biggest time thief, DISTRACTION.

Step 1 – Get a Journal and Calendar. You are going to use the journal to write out what your focal points are. Use the calendar as your active "To Do" list of daily activities you need to accomplish. Time management is key here, so you should schedule out EVERYTHING, so all time is accounted for.

TIP: Always schedule out your "Down" time as well, which is time dedicated just for you. This is to include time with family, catching a movie or just relaxing at home on your couch.

Step 2 – Keep it Front View. I LOVE to use Index cards. (Don't judge me.) I make index cards based on some of the things I really need to be reminded of daily and I place them EVERYWHERE, to include the bathroom mirror, above the kitchen sink, the closet and even by the front door under the key rack. With your goal of interest in your constant view, it becomes a form of meditation and you will think on it without effort. Get key quotes and scriptures that are relevant to your goal as well, to include books to read because reading trains the brain to focus.

TIP: When focusing and get knocked off course, have a plan of recourse *IN PLACE* to regain the focus. Don't get discouraged just keep going. Works, like a charm.

Step 3 – Get A Friend. It is important to have someone that checks in on you or someone you can call and just say, Hey! Let someone know that you may need help staying on tasks, so they can check up on you from time to time. Or, you can suggest calling them as your tasks are completed as a method of check in.

Whenever something goes wrong, the first thing I think is … what started this? Where did this begin and how did I get here. I seek to identify a solid root or seed so it can be uprooted or chopped down. The exposure of the root to your situations will effortlessly lead you into victory.

ACTION PLAN HERE

Write out your strengths

    1. _____
    2. _____
    3. _____
    4. _____
    5. _____

Write out your weaknesses

    1. _____
    2. _____

List 3 goals you want to accomplish this year. (Doesn't matter what month you are currently in this still applies.)

1. _____
2. _____
3. _____

<u>Now, write down 5 steps that you can take towards those 3 previous goals starting this week</u>

1. _____
2. _____
3. _____
4. _____
5. _____

Each week I want you to add a set of action steps until you achieve and accomplish your overall goals. The choice you make from this step forward will impact you forever. Make the CHOICE to Choose Life.

CONGRATULATIONS!!! I AM EXCITED ABOUT YOUR FUTURE!!!

<u>Words of Encouragement from The Author:</u>

I want to say I am proud of you for taking a step towards changing the course of your life. The journey is not easy but it's more than worth it. I went through many seasons of despair feeling like no matter what I did, I just couldn't break free from the life I knew. To say I felt *Stuck* to me still almost belittles the pain I felt from my life ending up at a dead end, no matter what routes I took. I realized when I got out, the routes were all the same, just different scenery.

The problem wasn't the route, it was the destination. Renewing my mind to the truth of what God had to say about me caused me to choose a different destination that ultimately impacted the route I took. It will take time to walk out your process BUT your decision is instant. As soon as you decide with your heart what you want to do, God immediately makes His presence known. He is always there, awaiting you.

The Lord told me to tell you this strategy.

When you feel Stuck, like you can't move, like your world is coming to an end, like you can't breathe and like you don't want to be HERE anymore.... DO THIS....

REMEMBER YOUR LAST VICTORY!

Remember the last time you felt like you weren't going to make it but then you did. The times you thought it would fail but it worked. The times when there was no natural way possible in a situation but then the supernatural God showed up. Remember Your Last Victory!!!

For those that may say, I feel like I haven't had any victories because life has just been hard. It's been one thing after the next, no peace.... I say to you, I have been there and know all too well what that feels like. A lot has to do with perspective. I have been sent to encourage you for brighter days. I know you have been hurt, discouraged and suffered periods of hopelessness. Those that you thought should be there weren't and you lost relationships along the way. I know...BUT here are the FACTS, ... things have been rough but the story is NOT OVER. You are here to express those feelings and tell the story. In critical moments in life, to know a person is still alive, they have to experience and demonstrate an emotion. The pain you feel indicates that your heart is beating. I'm here to tell you that Pain is Not your final Destination. Pick yourself up and TRY AGAIN, Dream again, Press again, LIVE again. You have nowhere to go but Up.

Let's Pray Together –

Father God, I thank you for this precious soul that has read this book. I thank you for the impartation of newness they have received and the injection of Faith that feels a little more tangible to them. I pray they align themselves with your will for their life and by your grace Father bring them from where they are now to the next level deeper in you. I thank you for changing their perspective and giving them a different way to think about their life with fresh perspective and new eyes. God, I release the Breaker's anointing upon the reader of this book right now and ask for a supernatural manifestation of your presence in their lives. Let them expect you in a way that allows you to Bless them and meet them at their hearts desire. Give them strength to do what only you can do and let them quickly see results of tangible change that will propel them forward. God, I thank you for them and pray their posture will now look to the hills from whence cometh their help. (Matthew 6:33) Hug them with your warm embrace, in Jesus Name. Amen!

DECLARATIONS AND PROCLAMATIONS

When you have received the Lord Jesus Christ as your personal Savior, you are entitled to the promises in the word of God. Below are some of my favorite scriptures, hope you like them.

DECLARATIONS...

Greater is He that is in me, than He that is in the world. (1 John 4:4)

I can do ALL things through Jesus Christ that gives me strength. (Philippians 4:13)

The Lord will never leave me nor forsake me. (Hebrews 13:5)

Lord, with You NOTHING is Impossible. (Luke 1:37)

Lord, it IS You that gives me the Power to get wealth. (Duet 8:18)

I will sleep peacefully at night and not be kept awake by restlessness and insomnia. (Psalm 3:5)

I will submit myself unto God, I will resist the enemy and he will flee. (James 4:7-8

PROMISES...

Lord, you promised if I obey you that I will have plenty to eat. (Isaiah 1:19)

Lord, you said you will supply all my need according to YOUR riches in glory, (Philippians 4:19)

If I delight myself in you, you will grant me the desires of my heart. (Psalm 37:4)

Lord, I thank you for the covenant agreement you made with me through Abraham… that I will be blessed and bless others. (Genesis 12:2)

Lord, I thank you that you conceal and hide me in your refuge, that you protect me and will deliver me from my enemies. (Psalm 91)

PROCLAIM…

I turn every curse sent my way into a Blessing. (Nehemiah 13:2)

I am chosen by God and I am Blessed! (Psalm 65:4)

I shall decree a thing and it shall be established. (Job 22:28)

I will teach my children of the Lord and they shall live in peace. (Isaiah 54:13)

My latter will be greater than my former. (Job 42:12)

This is my set time for Favor! (Psalm 102:12)

SPECIAL OFFER

As a Coach - Consultant, I assist in the process of personal and professional development. I provide strategies on how to engage your purpose in life, how to utilize your natural God given gifting's and how to achieve your maximum potential. In this process, we identify roadblocks, their roots, how to hurdle challenges, set plans in place and get you to achieve your goal.

I'm here to walk with you, encourage you, hold you accountable and push you past your comfort zone. I will stretch you, but it's all to enhance and improve the quality of your life. As a gift to you on your new journey, I am offering your first 30-minute session at a 75% discount, with proof of individual purchase.

After reading the book, we will go over what you feel is the biggest challenge you are currently facing and a method to approach it. It's simple, all you have to do is:

1) Send an email to kiyannibryan@gmail.com, with the following Subject Line "CL2K17"
2) Attach of a copy of your Full receipt for payment, and name.

You're all set.!!! Someone will get back with you with scheduling a time most convenient for you to chat.
I'm excited about your new journey and look forward to meeting you.

Kiyanni

(Disclaimer: The 75% discount is valid for "initial" 30 minute sessions only, and applied to the price of the session at the time of booking the appointment. Sessions are only permitted to approved potential clients, we reserve the right to deny clients based on our standards of values, moral and integrity.)

CONTACT INFO -

INVEST IN YOU BY STAYING CONNECTED

Kiyanni S. Bryan
Empowerment Coach & Solutions Strategist

Facebook Pages: Kiyanni S. Bryan

Instagram:	@kiyannib
Twitter:	@kiyannib
Periscope:	@kiyannib
YouTube:	Kiyanni S. Bryan
Website:	www.kiyannibryan.com
Email:	info@kiyannibryan.com

9780692886038